The Digital Equilibrium

Navigating Technological
Advancement for Optimal Well-Being

Shaurav Khadka

The Digital Equilibrium

Kindle Direct Publishing

The Digital Equilibrium:

Navigating Technological Advancement for Optimal Well-Being

Shaurav Khadka

Acknowledgments

I would like to express my heartfelt gratitude to all those who contributed to the creation of this book, "The Digital Equilibrium". This journey would not have been possible without the support, guidance, and encouragement of numerous individuals and resources.

I extend my appreciation to kindle direct publishing for providing a platform that enabled me to bring this project to fruition.

My sincere thanks go to calibre, google docs, photoshop and libre office for their robust tools, allowing me to seamlessly draft, edit, and refine the manuscript.

To my parents and sister, I am deeply grateful for your unwavering support and belief in my creative pursuits. Also, deep thanks to all my relatives who genuinely stick by my side. Your encouragement, patience, and understanding were invaluable as I navigated the intricate world of writing, technology, and well-being.

Lastly, I extend my gratitude to the readers, whose engagement and curiosity inspire me to explore the depths of digital well-being. Thank you, each and every one, for being a part of this endeavor.

Warmly,
Shaurav Khadka

The Digital Equilibrium

Disclaimer

The creation of this book was a collaborative endeavor that blended the capabilities of advanced artificial intelligence technology with the insights, direction, and editing provided by its powerful and imaginative creator. The driving force behind the book's content was a series of research-based prompts provided by the author, artificial intelligence, to help me create ideas for the chapters, sections, and paragraphs that comprise this comprehensive exploration of digital well-being.

The process began with the author's interest in the field of modern technology and health care, research and providing thoughtful prompts for each upcoming questions and doubts that arose during the whole process, outlining the topics they wanted to cover and the specific aspects they wished to delve into.

The research questions and prompts were carefully crafted with intensive brainstorming sessions to progress the entire journey of writing along with utilization of natural language processing artificial intelligence technology in content that aligned with the author's goals for the book. Their expertise and interests, played a significant role in shaping the content of this book. From discussing the impact of technology on mental health to exploring ethical considerations in the digital age, the research journey spanned a wide range of topics within the realm of digital well-being.

After completion of the initial draft based on the intensive research, evaluation, testing and conclusion, Author undertook the task of editing and refining the material to best reflect their vision and expertise. This editing process involved honing the language, structure, and flow of the content to ensure clarity, coherence, and accuracy. Through careful review and refinement, they ensured that the book's content met their high standards and effectively communicated the ideas and insights they intended to convey.

It's important to note that while artificial intelligence helped to generate the initial content based on the prompts, the final version of the book was shaped and polished by the my expertise, editorial insights, and dedication to presenting a comprehensive and valuable exploration of digital well-being. This collaborative process demonstrates the synergy between advanced artificial intelligence technology and human expertise, resulting in a book that encapsulates the individual's insights, passions, and commitment to the topic of digital well-being.

Legal Disclaimer

The information provided in this book is intended solely for informational and illustrative purposes. It is not intended to serve as comprehensive research or professional advice on any subject matter. The content within this book, including text, examples, images and insights were a careful and exploring journey in the realm of artificial general intelligence technology, which is offered as a showcase of the capabilities of modern technology and artificial intelligence. It should not be relied upon as a substitute for seeking professional guidance, consultation, or independent research.

The author, their tools, and the artificial general intelligence technologies used to help create this book do not assume any liability or responsibility for the accuracy, completeness, or applicability of the information provided in this book. While efforts have been made to ensure that the content is as accurate and up-to-date as possible, errors, omissions, and inaccuracies may occur. Some of the information presented may be outdated or incorrect.

Readers are advised to exercise their own judgment, discretion, and critical thinking when interpreting and applying the content within this book. The author and artificial intelligence technology provider do not endorse, warrant, or guarantee the reliability, validity, or completeness of the

Chapter 1: Foundations of Digital Well-Being

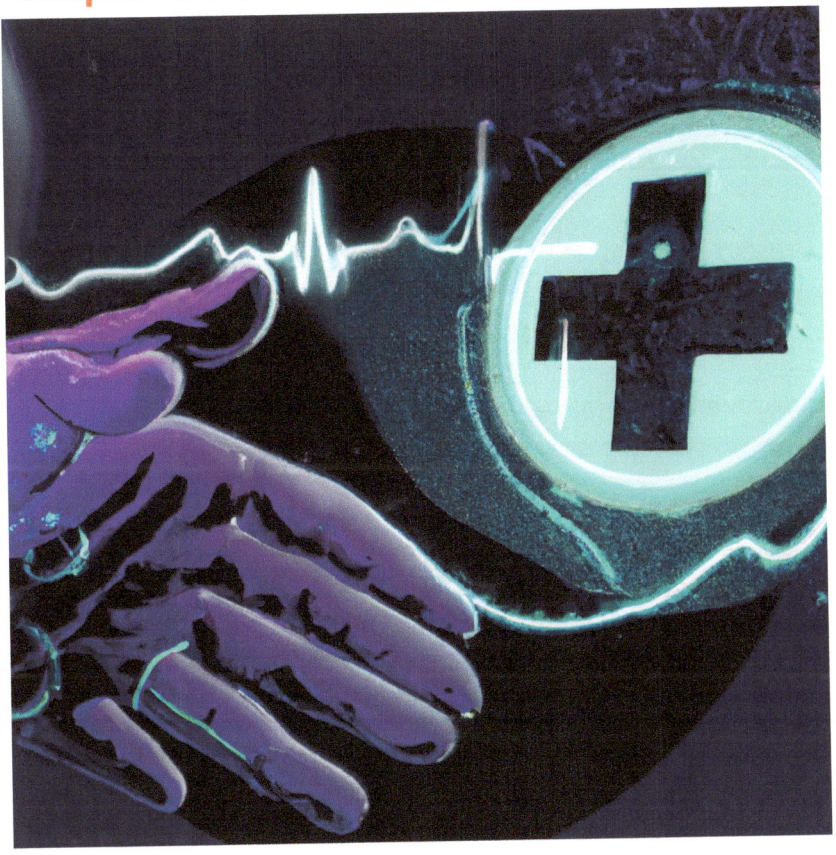

In a world propelled by relentless technological progress, our lives have become intricately intertwined with the digital realm. This chapter sets the stage for a comprehensive exploration of "Digital Well-Being," an emerging concept that demands our attention in the face of unprecedented connectivity. As we navigate this new era, understanding the fundamental principles underlying our relationship with technology is crucial. This chapter delves into the core tenets of digital well-being, shedding light on the psychological, emotional, and societal factors that shape our interactions with the digital landscape. By establishing a strong foundation of knowledge, we can begin to unravel the complexities of this multifaceted domain and pave the way for a more balanced and harmonious coexistence with technology.

As the digital age accelerates and permeates every facet of our lives, the concept of digital well-being emerges as a vital response to the challenges and opportunities presented by technology. This concept signifies more than just a fleeting trend; it embodies a profound shift in our perspective towards the digital landscape. In a world where smartphones are practically extensions of our hands and social media is a constant backdrop to our thoughts, we find ourselves facing an urgent need to examine how these advancements affect our mental, emotional, and physical well-being. The digital realm, with its boundless opportunities and intricate pitfalls, demands a thoughtful and strategic approach to ensure that our engagement with technology enhances rather than detracts from our overall quality of life.

Technology's profound influence on society is undeniable, and as we navigate this uncharted terrain, it becomes evident that the boundaries between the digital and the physical are becoming increasingly blurred. From social interactions to work environments, entertainment to education, our interactions with technology are inextricably woven into the fabric of our daily existence. This evolution prompts us to question not only the impact of technology on our well-being, but also the ways in which we can harness its potential to cultivate a more enriching and fulfilling life experience. By embracing the principles of digital well-being, we gain the tools to navigate this intricate landscape and channel technology's transformative power towards our benefit.

In the pursuit of digital well-being, it is imperative to recognize that our relationship with technology is multifaceted and dynamic. On one hand, we have the incredible convenience and efficiency that technology affords us, enabling us to connect with loved ones across the globe, access vast repositories of information at our fingertips, and automate various tasks for increased productivity. On the other hand, we encounter the potential pitfalls of excessive screen time, digital addiction, information overload, and privacy concerns. This juxtaposition underscores the need for a balanced and informed approach to digital engagement—one that empowers us to harness the advantages while mitigating the risks.

The journey towards digital well-being demands a departure from passive consumption towards intentional interaction. This shift entails understanding our digital habits, assessing their impact on our mental and emotional states, and making conscious choices to align our behaviors with our broader well-being goals. Moreover, as technology continues to evolve at an exponential pace, the narrative of digital well-being must remain adaptive and responsive. What constitutes a healthy digital lifestyle today may require adjustments tomorrow, making ongoing self-awareness and learning essential components of this journey.

In the chapters to come, we will dissect the intricacies of digital well-being, drawing insights from psychology, sociology, user experience design, ethics, and more. By delving into the heart of this topic, we aim to equip you with the knowledge and tools necessary to navigate the digital landscape with confidence and mindfulness. With a foundation rooted in understanding, we can embark on a transformative exploration of how to thrive in the digital age while preserving our mental, emotional, and physical well-being.

At the crossroads of technology and human psychology lies a complex interplay that shapes our overall well-being in ways both profound and intricate. In an era where screens pervade our daily lives and algorithms curate our online experiences, understanding the dynamic relationship between technology, psychology, and well-being is paramount. This chapter delves deep into this intersection, uncovering the psychological mechanisms that underlie our interactions with technology and their profound implications on our mental and emotional states.

Technology's omnipresence and its influence on human behavior raise intriguing questions about how our minds navigate this digital landscape. At the heart of this exploration lies the concept of psychological design—how interfaces, apps, and platforms are intentionally crafted to capture and sustain our attention. By tapping into principles from psychology, such as variable rewards and social validation, technology companies shape user behavior and engagement patterns. This manipulation of psychological triggers gives rise to addictive behaviors and a cycle of compulsive technology use that can affect our overall well-being.

Central to understanding the impact of technology on our well-being is the concept of the digital dopamine loop. As we receive notifications, likes, and messages, our brains release dopamine—a neurotransmitter associated with pleasure and reward. This creates a loop where we seek out digital interactions to experience the pleasurable dopamine release. However, this perpetual cycle can lead to addictive behaviors, anxiety, and reduced focus, ultimately affecting our mental and emotional health. Recognizing this dynamic allows us to approach technology with heightened awareness and make conscious choices about its role in our lives.

Moreover, the rise of social media has transformed the way we perceive ourselves and others, giving rise to the phenomenon of social comparison. Constant exposure to curated representations of others' lives can lead to feelings of inadequacy, envy, and a distorted sense of reality. This "highlight reel" effect can contribute to lower self-esteem and diminished overall well-being. Acknowledging the psychological impact of social media encourages us to foster a healthier relationship with online interactions and cultivate a sense of self-worth that isn't tied to external validation.

Beyond individual psychology, technology's influence extends to interpersonal dynamics and relationships. Digital communication platforms offer unparalleled connectivity, but they can also dilute the richness of face-to-face interactions. The absence of nonverbal cues, such as body language and tone of voice, can lead to misinterpretations and misunderstandings, potentially straining relationships. This highlights the need for digital communication literacy and the importance of balancing virtual connections with meaningful in-person interactions for sustained emotional well-being.

The phenomenon of "technostress" emerges as a significant factor at the nexus of technology and mental health. The constant influx of information, notifications, and demands from digital devices can lead to a state of chronic stress, impacting our ability to relax, concentrate, and disconnect. Understanding the sources of technostress—from email overload to digital multitasking—enables us to adopt coping strategies that mitigate its negative effects and promote a healthier digital lifestyle.

The concepts of "FOMO" (Fear of Missing Out) and "nomophobia" (the fear of being without a mobile device) shed light on the psychological underpinnings of our attachment to technology. These phenomena reveal the extent to which technology has become intertwined with our identity and sense of belonging. By recognizing the drivers of these anxieties, we can make conscious efforts to regain control over our digital habits and prioritize real-life experiences that contribute to our overall well-being.

In the realm of psychology, the concept of "flow" offers insights into the positive side of technology engagement. Flow is a state of optimal experience characterized by deep engagement and a sense of timelessness. Technology can facilitate flow experiences through interactive apps, creative platforms, and immersive virtual environments. Recognizing how technology can contribute to moments of positive absorption empowers us to harness its potential for enhancing well-being.

As we navigate this intricate landscape, it's clear that the intersection of technology, psychology, and well-being is a dynamic terrain that demands ongoing exploration and adaptation. By delving into the psychological mechanisms that drive our digital behaviors and examining their impact on our mental and emotional states, we equip ourselves with the tools needed to cultivate a balanced and intentional relationship with technology—one that aligns with our broader well-being goals.

The significance of understanding the intersection of technology, psychology, and overall well-being lies in our ability to navigate the digital landscape with intentionality and mindfulness. As technology continues to evolve and integrate more deeply into our lives, its effects on our mental and emotional health become increasingly pronounced. By delving into the psychological underpinnings of our digital behaviors, we gain insight into the mechanisms that drive our interactions with technology, allowing us to make informed decisions about its role in our lives.

One crucial aspect of this significance is the empowerment it offers in combating the potential negative impacts of excessive technology use. Armed with an understanding of concepts such as the digital dopamine loop, social comparison, and technostress, individuals are better equipped to recognize the signs of unhealthy digital habits. This awareness provides the foundation for implementing strategies that mitigate the adverse effects of technology on mental well-being. By acknowledging the psychological triggers that lead to compulsive behavior, we can exercise greater control over our digital consumption and allocate time more intentionally to activities that contribute to our overall happiness and fulfillment.

In essence, the significance of delving into the intersection of technology, psychology, and well-being lies in our ability to adapt and thrive in a digital age. By leveraging insights from psychology, we can develop a nuanced understanding of our relationship with technology and harness its potential for positive impact. This knowledge enables us to make choices that align with our values and aspirations, fostering a harmonious coexistence with technology that enhances rather than diminishes our overall well-being.

Chapter 2: The Impact of Hyperconnectivity

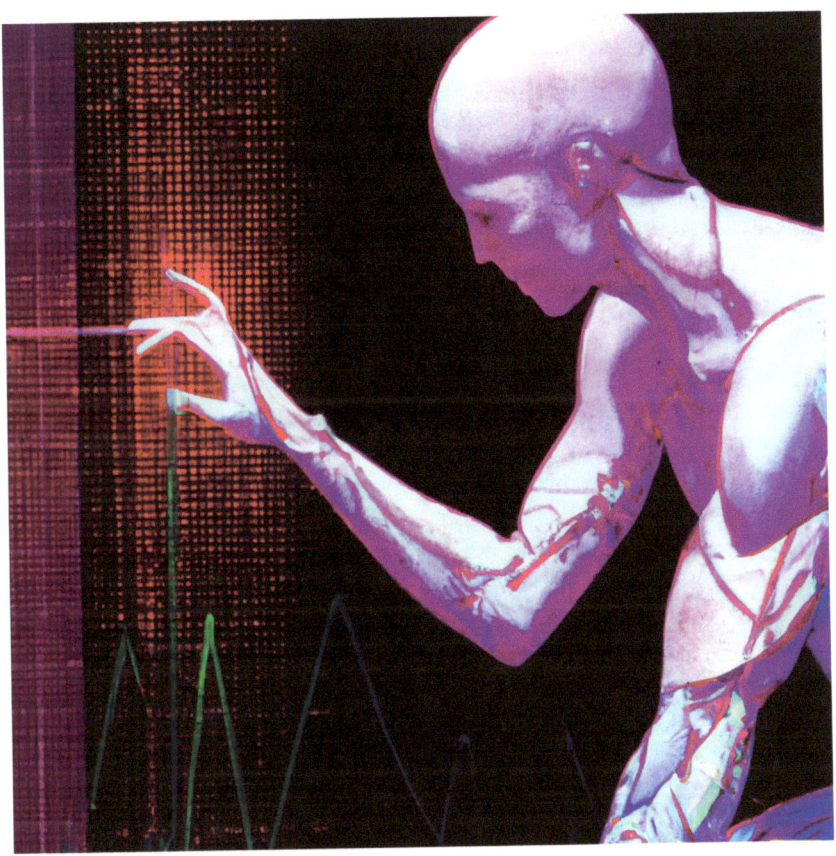

In a world where the pulse of digital connectivity reverberates ceaselessly, the concept of hyperconnectivity emerges as a defining feature of our modern lives. This chapter delves deep into the intricate web of connections that bind us to a global network, exploring the multifaceted impact of hyperconnectivity on our mental, social, and emotional well-being. As screens become the windows through which we engage with the world, it is imperative to dissect the implications of this constant connectedness, from its potential to foster meaningful connections to its capacity to amplify feelings of isolation and disconnection. By examining both the benefits and challenges of hyperconnectivity, we unravel the complex tapestry of our digital interactions and equip ourselves with the knowledge to navigate this brave new digital landscape with clarity and insight.

The ever-present allure of digital connectivity has revolutionized the way we communicate, work, and navigate our daily lives. However, this chapter delves into the underexplored realm of its impact on mental health and relationships, revealing a complex and often paradoxical landscape. On one hand, the ability to connect instantaneously with people across the globe has fostered a sense of global community and enabled unprecedented access to information. On the other hand, the unrelenting stream of notifications, messages, and updates has given rise to a state of perpetual distraction that can strain our mental resources and hamper our emotional well-being.

In the realm of mental health, the consequences of constant connectivity are multifaceted. The incessant exposure to curated online personas and the phenomenon of "social comparison" can contribute to feelings of inadequacy, anxiety, and even depression. The pressure to maintain a flawless digital facade can create a dichotomy between our online selves and our authentic identities, leading to a sense of disconnection from our own lives. Moreover, the constant bombardment of information and stimuli can lead to cognitive overload and reduced attention spans, affecting our ability to concentrate and engage deeply with tasks—a phenomenon known as "continuous partial attention."

The implications extend to the domain of relationships as well. While technology has the potential to bridge geographical distances and strengthen connections, it can also introduce barriers to authentic human interaction. The prevalence of digital communication platforms, while convenient, lacks the nuances of face-to-face conversations. This can lead to misunderstandings, misinterpretations, and a sense of emotional detachment. The temptation to resort to text-based communication over genuine conversations can erode the depth and intimacy of relationships, as nonverbal cues and emotional subtleties are lost in translation.

Furthermore, the addictive nature of digital devices can foster a constant state of "technoference," where the intrusion of technology into personal interactions undermines the quality of relationships. The compulsion to check devices during meals, conversations, and intimate moments can detract from the present moment and compromise the sense of connection with others. This fragmentation of attention can erode the bonds that thrive on genuine engagement, active listening, and shared experiences.

In navigating this terrain, it's crucial to recognize the need for intentional boundaries that protect mental well-being and nurture meaningful relationships. Setting aside designated periods for digital detoxification, where screens are silenced and connections are human-centric, can offer respite from the constant barrage of information. Embracing mindful practices that promote present-moment awareness can counteract the tendency to be constantly drawn into digital distractions. Ultimately, by critically analyzing the effects of constant connectivity on mental health and relationships, we empower ourselves to make conscious choices that prioritize authentic interactions, foster emotional well-being, and preserve the richness of human connection in a digitally saturated world.

The ever-present allure of digital connectivity has revolutionized the way we communicate, work, and navigate our daily lives. However, this chapter delves into the underexplored realm of its impact on mental health and relationships, revealing a complex and often paradoxical landscape. On one hand, the ability to connect instantaneously with people across the globe has fostered a sense of global community and enabled unprecedented access to information. On the other hand, the unrelenting stream of notifications, messages, and updates has given rise to a state of perpetual distraction that can strain our mental resources and hamper our emotional well-being.

In the realm of mental health, the consequences of constant connectivity are multifaceted. The incessant exposure to curated online personas and the phenomenon of "social comparison" can contribute to feelings of inadequacy, anxiety, and even depression. The pressure to maintain a flawless digital facade can create a dichotomy between our online selves and our authentic identities, leading to a sense of disconnection from our own lives. Moreover, the constant bombardment of information and stimuli can lead to cognitive overload and reduced attention spans, affecting our ability to concentrate and engage deeply with tasks—a phenomenon known as "continuous partial attention."

The implications extend to the domain of relationships as well. While technology has the potential to bridge geographical distances and strengthen connections, it can also introduce barriers to authentic human interaction. The prevalence of digital communication platforms, while convenient, lacks the nuances of face-to-face conversations. This can lead to misunderstandings, misinterpretations, and a sense of emotional detachment. The temptation to resort to text-based communication over genuine conversations can erode the depth and intimacy of relationships, as nonverbal cues and emotional subtleties are lost in translation.

Furthermore, the addictive nature of digital devices can foster a constant state of "technoference," where the intrusion of technology into personal interactions undermines the quality of relationships. The compulsion to check devices during meals, conversations, and intimate moments can detract from the present moment and compromise the sense of connection with others. This fragmentation of attention can erode the bonds that thrive on genuine engagement, active listening, and shared experiences.

In navigating this terrain, it's crucial to recognize the need for intentional boundaries that protect mental well-being and nurture meaningful relationships. Setting aside designated periods for digital detoxification, where screens are silenced and connections are human-centric, can offer respite from the constant barrage of information. Embracing mindful practices that promote present-moment awareness can counteract the tendency to be constantly drawn into digital distractions. Ultimately, by critically analyzing the effects of constant connectivity on mental health and relationships, we empower ourselves to make conscious choices that prioritize authentic interactions, foster emotional well-being, and preserve the richness of human connection in a digitally saturated world.

Chapter 3: Data Privacy and Personal Agency

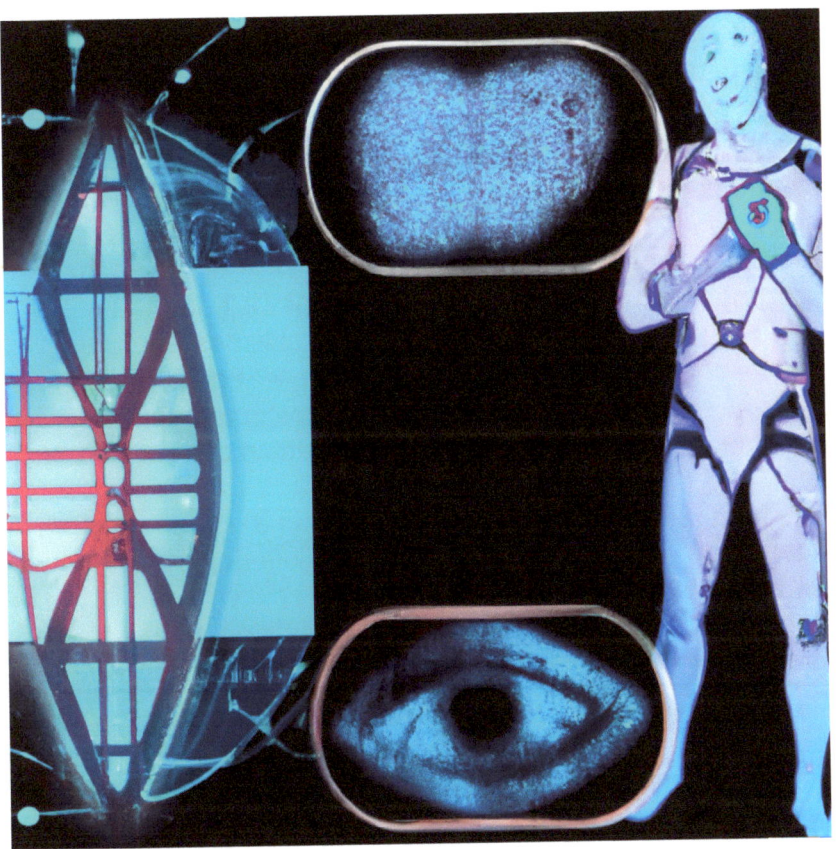

In the digital age, the exchange of information has become the currency of our interactions, powering the services and conveniences that shape our lives. Yet, with each click, swipe, and interaction, we leave behind a trail of personal data that holds the potential to shape our experiences in ways both empowering and concerning. This chapter dives into the pivotal realm of data privacy and personal agency, examining the intricate interplay between our digital footprints and the preservation of our individual autonomy. As we navigate a landscape where data is harvested, analyzed, and monetized, understanding the nuances of data privacy is paramount. By delving into topics such as consent, surveillance, and the ethical considerations of data collection, we equip ourselves with the tools needed to assert control over our personal information and navigate the digital world on our own terms.

In an era where information flows freely and digital interactions are woven into the fabric of our daily routines, data privacy emerges as a fundamental concern that underpins our digital citizenship. The vast amount of personal data generated through our online activities—from search queries and social media posts to shopping habits and location data—paints a detailed portrait of who we are, what we value, and how we navigate the world. Understanding the importance of data privacy is not merely an exercise in safeguarding personal secrets; it is a pivotal step toward preserving individual agency, preventing unauthorized exploitation, and maintaining a sense of control over the digital realm.

One of the primary drivers behind the importance of data privacy lies in the potential for misuse and unauthorized access. As data becomes a valuable commodity, it attracts not only legitimate organizations seeking to enhance their services but also malicious actors seeking to exploit vulnerabilities for financial gain or even political influence. The accumulation of disparate pieces of personal information can create a comprehensive profile that can be manipulated to target individuals with tailored advertisements, scams, or even manipulation of opinions and beliefs. By safeguarding data privacy, individuals are better equipped to shield themselves from these risks and maintain their autonomy in the digital landscape.

Furthermore, data privacy intersects with ethical considerations surrounding consent and autonomy. With the ubiquity of data collection mechanisms, individuals often find themselves unwittingly contributing to the digital databases that power algorithmic decision-making, predictive analytics, and personalized recommendations. Understanding the implications of data sharing enables individuals to make informed choices about what information they are comfortable sharing and with whom. This informed consent is central to ensuring that personal agency is preserved in the face of ever-evolving technological advancements.

The implications of data privacy extend beyond personal autonomy to the broader societal implications of data aggregation and surveillance. The aggregation of vast amounts of data enables profiling and predictive modeling, with potential consequences for issues ranging from credit scoring to criminal justice decisions. Surveillance practices, both by governmental entities and private corporations, raise questions about civil liberties, human rights, and the potential for systemic bias. Acknowledging the importance of data privacy prompts discussions about the balance between security and personal freedoms and underscores the need for transparent, ethical, and accountable data practices.

Moreover, the digital world is characterized by the interplay between convenience and privacy. Services that offer seamless experiences—such as personalized recommendations, targeted advertisements, and location-based services—often come at the cost of sharing personal data. Recognizing the importance of data privacy requires individuals to assess the trade-offs between convenience and control, and to make deliberate choices that align with their values and comfort levels. This critical evaluation empowers individuals to engage with technology in a manner that enhances their well-being while minimizing potential risks.

In essence, the importance of data privacy transcends individual preferences to shape the broader landscape of digital interactions. By understanding the intricacies of data collection, consent, and utilization, individuals are better equipped to navigate the digital age on their own terms. Empowered with knowledge, they can actively participate in shaping a digital world that respects personal agency, upholds ethical standards, and preserves the principles of autonomy and individuality.

In a landscape where digital footprints are as ubiquitous as the paths we tread, the responsibility to protect our personal information has never been more paramount. This chapter not only delves into the intricacies of data privacy but also empowers readers with practical knowledge and strategies to safeguard their digital identities. Understanding the vulnerabilities of the digital landscape is the first step toward reclaiming agency over one's personal information and ensuring that the digital realm remains a space of empowerment rather than exploitation.

The journey toward safeguarding personal information begins with awareness—awareness of the data we generate through online activities, the platforms we engage with, and the potential risks associated with data sharing. By cultivating a clear understanding of the types of data that are collected, stored, and utilized, readers can make informed decisions about their online behaviors and the settings they choose to configure. From browsing history to geolocation data, every interaction contributes to the digital mosaic that defines our online presence.

Equipped with knowledge, readers can delve into the intricacies of privacy settings, encryption protocols, and consent mechanisms. Platforms often provide granular control over data sharing, allowing users to customize their level of engagement and the information they disclose. Learning to navigate these settings empowers readers to strike a balance between participating in the digital world and preserving their privacy. Encryption, too, plays a pivotal role in data protection. Understanding the basics of encryption and its role in securing online communications enables readers to adopt secure practices that shield sensitive information from prying eyes.

As digital footprints leave traces across a multitude of platforms, readers can also explore the concept of data minimization. This practice involves evaluating the necessity of sharing specific pieces of information and adopting a mindset of selective disclosure. By sharing only what is essential for a given transaction or interaction, individuals reduce the amount of data available for potential exploitation. This approach not only safeguards personal information but also fosters a sense of control and autonomy over the data that defines one's online persona.

Amidst the complexities of data privacy, readers can also explore the concept of "digital hygiene." Similar to physical hygiene practices that promote health, digital hygiene encompasses behaviors that protect online well-being. Regularly updating passwords, enabling two-factor authentication, and being cautious of phishing attempts are all components of digital hygiene that minimize the risk of data breaches and unauthorized access. Through proactive habits and informed decision-making, readers can fortify their digital defenses and navigate the online landscape with confidence.

The empowerment of protecting personal information extends to understanding the legal and regulatory landscape that governs data privacy. Readers can delve into frameworks such as the General Data Protection Regulation (GDPR) and the

California Consumer Privacy Act (CCPA), gaining insights into their rights as data subjects and the responsibilities of organizations that handle personal data. This knowledge not only enhances individual agency but also encourages advocacy for transparent and ethical data practices on a broader scale.

By empowering readers with the tools to protect their personal information, this chapter ensures that the digital world remains a space where agency and autonomy thrive. Armed with practical strategies, readers can confidently engage with technology, make informed decisions, and contribute to a digital ecosystem that respects privacy and champions individual rights. In a landscape defined by data flows and digital interactions, the ability to safeguard personal information becomes an act of empowerment, enabling individuals to shape their digital narratives on their own terms.

Chapter 4: Designing for User Wellness

In an era where technology is seamlessly integrated into every facet of our lives, the role of design extends beyond aesthetics to encompass its profound impact on user well-being. This chapter delves into the crucial realm of user experience (UX) design, exploring how thoughtful design principles can shape digital interactions to promote user wellness and enhance overall satisfaction. As technology becomes an extension of our senses and behaviors, understanding the ways in which design can influence our emotions, behaviors, and cognitive states is essential. By dissecting the principles of empathetic design, usability, and ethical considerations, this chapter equips readers with the tools needed to navigate a digital landscape that prioritizes user well-being and fosters positive engagement.

In the realm of technology, user experience (UX) design emerges as a driving force that shapes the way we interact with digital interfaces. Beyond aesthetics and functionality, UX design holds the power to influence our emotional states, cognitive processes, and overall satisfaction. This chapter delves into the profound impact of UX design on digital well-being, shedding light on the principles and strategies that designers employ to foster positive, meaningful, and enriching interactions. By crafting interfaces that prioritize user wellness and mitigate potential harms, UX designers play a pivotal role in shaping a digital landscape that enhances rather than hinders our mental and emotional states.

At the core of promoting digital well-being through UX design lies the principle of empathetic design. Understanding the diverse needs, behaviors, and emotions of users is a cornerstone of creating interfaces that resonate with their experiences. By embracing the perspectives of different user segments, designers can develop inclusive and accessible solutions that cater to a wide range of preferences and abilities. This empathetic approach ensures that digital interactions are not only functional but also considerate of the diverse emotional responses and well-being considerations of users.

Usability, another fundamental aspect of UX design, plays a vital role in reducing frustration and enhancing user well-being. Interfaces that are intuitive, easy to navigate, and responsive contribute to a seamless and positive user experience. By minimizing cognitive load and eliminating unnecessary complexities, designers enable users to engage with technology effortlessly, reducing stress and anxiety associated with confusing or counterintuitive interfaces. This focus on usability aligns with the broader goal of digital well-being by creating a frictionless environment that empowers users to accomplish their tasks with efficiency and confidence.

Ethical considerations in UX design are integral to promoting digital well-being, as designers bear the responsibility of shaping interactions that prioritize user interests and values. Design choices related to data privacy, transparency, and consent have profound implications for user trust and psychological well-being. Implementing features that allow users to control their data sharing, offering clear explanations of how data is used, and minimizing dark patterns that manipulate user behaviors are all ethical dimensions of design that contribute to a sense of empowerment and trust.

Furthermore, the concept of "persuasive design" highlights the ability of UX design to influence user behaviors in ways that align with their goals and well-being. By incorporating principles from behavioral psychology, designers can nudge users towards positive actions and habits. For example, incorporating visual cues that encourage moderation in screen time or implementing progress indicators that motivate users to complete tasks can foster a sense of achievement and well-being. This strategic alignment of design with user goals ensures that digital interactions are not only engaging but also supportive of individual aspirations.

Addressing potential addictive behaviors is another critical dimension of promoting digital well-being through UX design. By understanding the psychological triggers that lead to compulsive technology use, designers can implement features that promote healthy usage patterns. For instance, notifications that provide information without inducing anxiety, features that encourage breaks and time management, and settings that allow users to customize their levels of engagement all contribute to a balanced and mindful digital experience. This approach empowers users to harness the benefits of technology while minimizing its potential negative impact on mental and emotional health.

In essence, the role of user experience design in promoting digital well-being transcends aesthetics to encompass a holistic understanding of user needs, behaviors, and values.

By embracing empathetic design, usability, ethical considerations, persuasive techniques, and addressing addictive behaviors, designers contribute to a digital landscape that respects user agency, enhances emotional well-being, and fosters positive engagement. Through their creative expertise, designers shape a digital world that aligns with individual aspirations, promotes balanced usage, and supports the broader goal of fostering well-being in the age of technology.

Mindful design principles offer a framework that aligns user experience with well-being, fostering interactions that prioritize satisfaction, meaningful engagement, and emotional resonance. In this chapter, we delve into specific examples of how designers apply these principles to create interfaces that enhance user well-being, making digital interactions not only functional but also deeply satisfying.

1. Minimalist and Intuitive Interfaces:

Mindful design often emphasizes simplicity and clarity. Interfaces that employ minimalist design principles minimize visual clutter, prioritize essential elements, and guide users intuitively through tasks. By reducing cognitive load and making interactions straightforward, designers create an environment where users can engage with technology effortlessly and without undue stress.

2. Thoughtful Feedback and Microinteractions:

Designers can enhance user satisfaction by incorporating microinteractions—subtle animations, visual cues, and feedback that respond to user actions. These interactions provide a sense of immediacy and acknowledgment, which can be particularly impactful in applications that involve tasks like form submissions or button clicks. Thoughtful feedback enhances user confidence and emotional well-being by signaling successful interactions and maintaining a sense of continuity.

3. Personalization and Customization:

Empowering users to tailor their digital experiences is a hallmark of mindful design. Interfaces that allow users to personalize layouts, color schemes, and content preferences cater to individual tastes and preferences. This customization fosters a sense of ownership and control, promoting emotional well-being by aligning the interface with users' unique identities and needs.

4. Distraction Mitigation:

Mindful design considers the potential for distractions and employs strategies to mitigate them. For instance, in apps that encourage focused work or relaxation, designers may incorporate features that temporarily mute notifications or encourage users to take breaks. By supporting users in managing distractions and maintaining their cognitive focus, designers contribute to a sense of accomplishment and well-being.

5. Ethical Notifications and Time Management:

Mindful design extends to how notifications are employed. Designers can prioritize well-being by offering options that allow users to receive notifications at appropriate times and frequencies. Ethical considerations prompt designers to avoid tactics that induce urgency or addictive behaviors, fostering a balanced and intentional relationship with technology.

6. Inclusive Design for Diverse Users:

Inclusive design practices cater to a wide range of user abilities and needs. By incorporating features like alt text for images, clear typography, and resizable interfaces, designers ensure that digital experiences are accessible and respectful of diverse users. This inclusivity contributes to user satisfaction and emotional well-being by allowing everyone to engage with technology on their terms.

In sum, the application of mindful design principles offers a roadmap for enhancing user satisfaction and well-being. By prioritizing intuitive interfaces, thoughtful feedback, personalization, distraction management, ethical notifications, and inclusivity, designers create digital environments that resonate with users on a deeper level. These examples showcase the transformative potential of design in shaping digital interactions that enrich lives, foster meaningful engagement, and contribute to overall well-being.

Chapter 5: Mindful Consumption in the Digital Sphere

In an age of abundant information and constant connectivity, the act of consumption has evolved into a complex web of digital interactions that influence our thoughts, behaviors, and well-being. This chapter explores the concept of mindful consumption in the digital sphere, delving into the ways in which our choices, behaviors, and interactions with online content shape our cognitive landscape and emotional experiences. From social media feeds to news articles and entertainment platforms, the digital world presents a vast array of content that demands our attention and discernment. By examining strategies for cultivating mindfulness in our digital consumption habits, we embark on a journey to harness the potential of technology for enrichment, empowerment, and fostering a balanced relationship with the digital realm.

In an era where information is a constant companion, the phenomenon of information overload has emerged as a significant challenge that affects our cognitive well-being. The digital sphere inundates us with an overwhelming stream of news, updates, notifications, and content, making it increasingly difficult to sift through the noise and extract meaningful insights. This chapter delves into the consequences of information overload and digital clutter on cognitive health, examining how these factors can lead to cognitive fatigue, reduced attention spans, and even decision-making paralysis.

Information overload has profound implications for cognitive health, as the sheer volume of content vying for our attention taxes our cognitive resources. The constant exposure to stimuli, often accompanied by a sense of urgency, triggers the brain's stress response. This chronic state of arousal can lead to cognitive fatigue, making it harder to concentrate, process information, and make decisions. As our cognitive capacity becomes strained, our ability to engage in deep, focused thinking—essential for critical analysis and problem-solving—becomes compromised.

Digital clutter exacerbates the challenges posed by information overload. The digital landscape is replete with endless tabs, open apps, and unread emails—all competing for our attention. This clutter creates a fragmented mental space that inhibits our ability to focus on a single task. Moreover, the persistent presence of digital clutter heightens our cognitive load, overwhelming our working memory and impeding our capacity to retain and process new information. The resulting cognitive strain diminishes our overall cognitive health and can contribute to feelings of frustration and mental fatigue.

The impact of information overload and digital clutter extends beyond cognitive fatigue to reduced attention spans. The constant exposure to bite-sized, rapidly changing content—commonplace on social media platforms—conditions our brains to seek quick rewards and instant gratification. This phenomenon, known as "attention fragmentation," makes it challenging to engage with longer-form content, such as in-depth articles or books. As our attention spans shrink, we may find it difficult to engage in sustained, focused reading and critical thinking, hindering our ability to absorb complex ideas and deepen our understanding of subjects.

Furthermore, information overload and digital clutter can lead to decision-making paralysis. When faced with an abundance of options and information, individuals may become overwhelmed and struggle to make choices. This phenomenon is particularly evident in the digital realm, where the proliferation of choices—from products to content to online interactions—can leave individuals feeling paralyzed by the fear of making suboptimal decisions. This indecision not only impairs our ability to navigate the digital landscape efficiently but also contributes to heightened stress and reduced satisfaction with our choices.

To address the impact of information overload and digital clutter on cognitive health, cultivating mindfulness in digital consumption is paramount. Mindful consumption involves deliberate, purposeful engagement with content, allowing us to filter out noise and prioritize what truly matters to us. Implementing strategies such as setting specific time limits for digital engagement, unsubscribing from unnecessary email lists, and curating social media feeds to include only relevant and valuable content can help mitigate the negative effects of information overload and digital clutter.

In conclusion, the impact of information overload and digital clutter on cognitive health underscores the need for intentional, mindful consumption in the digital sphere. By recognizing the cognitive strain posed by excessive content and clutter, individuals can adopt strategies that promote focused attention, reduce cognitive fatigue, and enable more deliberate decision-making. As we navigate the digital landscape, cultivating mindfulness in our consumption habits becomes an essential tool for preserving cognitive well-being and harnessing the benefits of technology without succumbing to its pitfalls.

As the deluge of digital content continues unabated, the importance of curating our digital consumption becomes increasingly apparent. This chapter presents practical techniques that empower individuals to navigate the digital landscape with intentionality, fostering cognitive well-being, and promoting meaningful engagement.

1. Define Your Priorities:

Begin by clarifying your digital consumption priorities. What types of content are most valuable to you? Which platforms align with your interests and goals? By defining your priorities, you can focus your attention on content that truly enriches your life and filters out unnecessary noise.

2. Practice Unsubscribing and Unfollowing:

Regularly evaluate your subscriptions and social media follows. Unsubscribe from email lists that no longer provide value and unfollow accounts that do not contribute positively to your well-being. This practice streamlines your digital environment and ensures that you receive content that resonates with your interests.

3. Limit Multitasking:

Multitasking divides your attention and hampers cognitive efficiency. When consuming digital content, avoid the temptation to simultaneously engage in other tasks. Instead, allocate dedicated time for focused content consumption, allowing you to absorb information more deeply and retain it effectively.

4. Curate Your News Sources:

Diversify your sources of news and information to gain a well-rounded perspective. Follow reputable, balanced sources that prioritize accuracy and thoughtful analysis. Avoid echo chambers that reinforce preexisting beliefs and seek out platforms that challenge your perspectives.

5. Implement Information Fasting:

Just as periodic fasting benefits physical health, information fasting benefits cognitive health. Set designated periods during the day when you disconnect from digital devices. This practice offers mental respite, reduces cognitive overload, and allows your mind to recharge.

6. Adopt the Rule of Three:

When encountering new content, apply the rule of three: reflect on whether the information aligns with your values, contributes to your knowledge, or has a practical application in your life. If content fails to meet these criteria, consider skipping or discarding it.

By implementing these techniques, individuals can curate their digital content consumption to align with their values, interests, and cognitive well-being. The practice of mindful content curation empowers individuals to regain control over their digital interactions, fostering an environment that promotes meaningful engagement, critical thinking, and a balanced relationship with technology.

Chapter 6: Navigating Digital Distractions

In a world defined by constant connectivity and a barrage of digital stimuli, the challenge of navigating digital distractions has become a pervasive concern. This chapter delves into the multifaceted landscape of digital interruptions, exploring the sources of distractions and their profound implications on productivity, focus, and overall well-being. By dissecting the underlying causes of distractions and presenting strategies to regain focus and manage interruptions effectively, this chapter equips individuals with the tools needed to navigate the digital realm with intentionality, fostering a more purposeful and productive engagement with technology.

By dissecting these distractions and understanding their impact, individuals can develop strategies to regain control over their attention and achieve a more balanced relationship with technology.

Identifying Common Sources of Digital Distractions and Their Implications on Productivity:

1. Social Media Temptations:

Social media platforms are designed to capture and retain attention, often employing techniques such as infinite scrolling, notifications, and personalized content recommendations. The lure of continuously refreshing feeds and responding to notifications can result in fragmented attention, reducing productivity and compromising cognitive focus. For instance, a quick glance at a social media feed can easily snowball into minutes or even hours of aimless scrolling, detracting from more meaningful tasks.

2. Email Overload:

The incessant influx of emails vying for our attention can disrupt workflow and drain cognitive resources. Constant email checking can lead to a state of continuous partial attention, where individuals remain on high alert for incoming messages, even during tasks that require deep focus. This state of divided attention impedes productivity and can prolong task completion times. For example, toggling between a critical project and email responses can hinder cognitive engagement and hinder the quality of work.

3. Push Notifications:

Mobile apps and devices send a constant stream of push notifications, ranging from news updates to app notifications and instant messages. The Pavlovian response to these notifications can divert attention from tasks, disrupt concentration, and contribute to task-switching behaviors. A real-world scenario involves a student trying to study who gets sidetracked every time a notification pops up, diminishing study effectiveness.

4. Multitasking and Task Switching:

The allure of multitasking—attempting to juggle multiple tasks simultaneously—often results in reduced cognitive performance. Frequent task-switching fragments attention, leading to longer completion times for each task and a diminished ability to engage in deep, focused work. An example of this might be a professional attempting to manage emails, work on a presentation, and respond to instant messages all at once, resulting in lower quality output and a sense of mental fatigue.

5. Entertainment and Instant Gratification:

The allure of on-demand entertainment, such as streaming videos, games, and online content, can quickly lead to procrastination and distraction. The promise of immediate gratification competes with tasks that require sustained effort and cognitive engagement. For instance, a student aiming to complete an assignment might find themselves succumbing to the temptation of watching a TV show instead, delaying productive work.

Recognizing the implications of distractions such as social media, email overload, push notifications, multitasking, and instant gratification empowers individuals to develop strategies that mitigate their impact.

In the face of constant digital interruptions, individuals can adopt a range of strategies to regain control over their attention and promote productivity. By implementing mindful practices and technological adjustments, individuals can navigate the digital landscape with intentionality, fostering a balanced relationship with technology while achieving their goals.

1. Mindful Task Management:

Adopt techniques such as the Pomodoro Technique, where work is broken into focused intervals followed by short breaks. This approach helps structure work and rest periods, enhancing cognitive engagement and minimizing the allure of distractions. For example, a researcher aiming to write a report might dedicate 25-minute intervals to focused writing, followed by a brief break to check messages or take a walk.

2. Notification Management:

Take control of notifications by customizing settings to receive only essential alerts. Consider using "Do Not Disturb" modes during focused work periods. This practice curbs the impulse to immediately respond to every notification, enabling sustained attention and reducing the frequency of task-switching. A professional in a meeting might activate "Do Not Disturb" to ensure uninterrupted focus on the discussion.

3. Digital Detoxification:

Schedule designated periods to disconnect from digital devices entirely. Designating "offline" hours or days allows individuals to recharge, engage in non-screen activities, and cultivate mindfulness. An individual might choose to have a technology-free evening to read, engage in hobbies, or spend quality time with loved ones.

4. App and Website Blockers:

Utilize software tools that temporarily block distracting apps and websites during work or study periods. These blockers create a virtual barrier between individuals and their most common sources of distraction, facilitating focused work and reducing the temptation to deviate from tasks.

5. Establish Tech-Free Zones:

Designate specific areas, such as your bedroom or dining table, as tech-free zones. This creates boundaries between digital interactions and offline activities, fostering a healthier balance between technology use and relaxation.

6. Mindful Content Consumption:

Practice intentional content consumption by evaluating whether a piece of content aligns with your goals and interests before engaging with it. This approach prevents mindless scrolling and ensures that your digital interactions are purposeful and enriching.

By implementing these strategies, individuals can reclaim their attention from the clutches of digital distractions. The deliberate cultivation of focused attention and intentional digital engagement empowers individuals to strike a balance between the benefits of technology and the need for cognitive well-being. Navigating the digital landscape with purpose and mindfulness enables individuals to harness the potential of technology while maintaining control over their attention and productivity.

Chapter 7: Cultivating Digital Mindfulness

In a world characterized by constant connectivity and information saturation, the concept of digital mindfulness emerges as a guiding principle for navigating the digital landscape with intentionality and awareness. This chapter explores the profound practice of digital mindfulness, delving into its principles, benefits, and the transformative impact it can have on our cognitive well-being, emotional resilience, and overall quality of life. From fostering a conscious relationship with technology to developing self-awareness in our digital interactions, the journey of cultivating digital mindfulness offers individuals the tools to harness the benefits of technology while safeguarding their mental and emotional health. By embracing this practice, individuals can transform their digital experiences into sources of enrichment, clarity, and meaningful engagement.

Mindfulness, the practice of being fully present and attentive to the present moment, can be applied to our digital interactions to foster a healthier and more intentional relationship with technology.

1. Digital Breath Awareness:

Just as mindfulness often begins with focusing on the breath, digital breath awareness involves taking intentional breaths before engaging with digital devices. This practice creates a moment of pause, allowing individuals to transition from autopilot to conscious engagement. Before unlocking a device or opening an app, individuals can take a few deep breaths, centering their attention and setting a mindful tone for their digital interactions.

2. Purposeful Scrolling:

Mindful scrolling involves approaching social media and online content with intentionality. Before starting to scroll, individuals can ask themselves why they are engaging with the content and what they hope to gain from it. This practice prevents mindless scrolling and encourages individuals to engage with content that aligns with their values and interests, promoting a more meaningful online experience.

3. Digital Detox Moments:

Incorporating short digital detox moments throughout the day allows individuals to reset their attention and recenter their focus. During these moments, individuals step away from screens, engage in a short mindfulness meditation, or simply observe their surroundings. These pauses foster mental clarity, reduce cognitive fatigue, and enhance overall cognitive well-being in the midst of digital interactions.

4. Mindful App and Notification Management:

Mindful management of digital tools involves evaluating the purpose and impact of apps and notifications. Regularly assess which apps and notifications truly contribute positively to your well-being and goals. Uninstall or mute those that detract from your focus and peace of mind. This practice ensures that your digital environment supports mindfulness and intentional engagement.

By integrating these tailored mindfulness practices into the digital era, individuals can navigate the digital landscape with greater awareness and purpose. These practices empower individuals to approach technology mindfully, cultivating a harmonious balance between the benefits of digital interactions and the preservation of mental clarity and well-being.

In the realm of online interactions, cultivating awareness and intentionality requires conscious efforts to engage with digital platforms in ways that align with our values and well-being.

1. Mindful Posting and Commenting:

Before posting or commenting on social media, take a moment to reflect on the intention behind your words. Ask yourself if your contribution adds value, promotes positive discourse, or resonates with your authentic voice. This practice encourages thoughtful and respectful interactions, fostering a virtual environment that nourishes well-being and meaningful connections.

2. Digital Boundary Setting:

Setting clear boundaries for your online interactions is crucial for maintaining mindfulness. Define specific time periods for checking emails and social media, and avoid engaging in work-related tasks outside of designated hours. This practice prevents the encroachment of digital interactions into personal time, fostering a healthier balance between online and offline experiences.

3. Mindful Content Consumption:

Apply mindfulness principles to your content consumption habits. When engaging with news, articles, or videos, be discerning about the sources and the emotional impact of the content. Avoid mindless scrolling and instead choose to engage with content that enriches your understanding, challenges your perspectives, or brings joy and inspiration.

By embracing these techniques, individuals can infuse their online interactions with mindfulness, intentionality, and a deeper sense of purpose. These practices empower individuals to navigate the digital realm with heightened awareness, fostering connections, preserving cognitive clarity, and fostering a sense of fulfillment amidst the sea of online experiences.

Chapter 8: Balancing Work and Screen Time

The increasing integration of digital technology into professional endeavors has brought about new challenges in maintaining a healthy balance between work and screen time. In this chapter, we delve into the intricate dynamics of achieving equilibrium between professional commitments and the demands of digital interactions. From remote work arrangements to virtual collaboration, the digital age offers unprecedented flexibility and connectivity, but also presents the risk of blurred boundaries and digital burnout. This chapter explores strategies to establish boundaries, prioritize well-being, and cultivate a harmonious relationship between work-related screen time and the need for rest, rejuvenation, and meaningful offline experiences.

The digital age has ushered in a new era of connectivity, allowing individuals to work, collaborate, and communicate across geographical boundaries. However, this digital connectivity has also given rise to challenges that can disrupt the delicate balance between work responsibilities and personal well-being.

1. Permeable Boundaries:

The lines between work and personal life can blur when technology facilitates constant access to work-related tasks and communications. With emails, messages, and virtual meetings accessible at all hours, individuals may find it difficult to disengage from work and dedicate time to personal pursuits, relaxation, and quality time with loved ones.

2. Digital Overload:

The proliferation of digital devices and platforms can lead to information overload, resulting in cognitive fatigue and reduced effectiveness in both work and personal activities. The constant barrage of notifications and information can contribute to feelings of overwhelm, making it challenging to disconnect and recharge.

3. Virtual Presenteeism:

The expectation of being virtually present at all times, even outside of traditional work hours, can lead to a culture of virtual presenteeism. This phenomenon pressures individuals to respond to messages and emails promptly, regardless of their personal circumstances. This pressure can erode the boundaries between work and personal life, impacting mental well-being and diminishing the quality of off-screen experiences.

4. FOMO and Social Comparison:

The digital realm offers glimpses into the professional achievements and experiences of others, often triggering feelings of Fear of Missing Out (FOMO) and social comparison. This can lead to an unrelenting need to stay connected and stay informed, even at the expense of personal downtime. The pursuit of career advancement and the fear of missing out on opportunities can lead to overcommitment and neglect of personal well-being.

5. Digital Burnout:

The cumulative effect of these challenges can contribute to digital burnout, a state of mental, emotional, and physical exhaustion resulting from prolonged and excessive screen time. Digital burnout can manifest as reduced productivity, increased irritability, and diminished engagement in both work and personal life. Striking a balance between work and screen time becomes imperative to mitigate the risk of burnout and preserve overall well-being.

In essence, the challenges of maintaining work-life balance in a digitally connected world require a proactive approach that encompasses setting boundaries, managing digital overload, resisting the pressure of virtual presenteeism, fostering resilience against FOMO and social comparison, and guarding against the onset of digital burnout. By recognizing these challenges, individuals can cultivate strategies to protect their well-being, establish healthier relationships with digital technology, and ensure that their professional pursuits harmonize with the richness of their personal lives.

Striking a balance between productivity and well-being in a digitally connected world requires a deliberate and holistic approach that empowers individuals to make intentional choices and create a harmonious rhythm between work and personal life.

1. Establish Clear Boundaries:

Defining distinct boundaries between work and personal time is crucial. Set specific hours for work-related tasks and communication, and communicate these boundaries to colleagues and supervisors. This practice helps protect personal time for relaxation, hobbies, and quality interactions with family and friends.

2. Embrace Digital Sabbaticals:

Regularly disconnecting from digital devices and work-related activities through intentional "digital sabbaticals" can provide much-needed respite. Dedicate periods of time—whether it's a few hours, a full day, or a weekend—to disconnecting from work-related tasks, allowing yourself to recharge and engage in offline activities that bring joy and relaxation.

3. Prioritize Self-Care:

Incorporating self-care practices into your routine is essential for maintaining well-being. Engage in activities that promote physical health, mental clarity, and emotional balance, such as exercise, meditation, journaling, and spending time in nature. Prioritizing self-care not only enhances your overall well-being but also boosts your productivity and focus when engaged in work tasks.

4. Practice Mindful Work Habits:

Infuse mindfulness into your work habits by cultivating present-moment awareness while performing tasks. Mindful work involves focusing your attention fully on the task at hand, minimizing distractions, and avoiding multitasking. By immersing yourself in each task, you enhance your efficiency, reduce errors, and foster a sense of accomplishment, contributing to your overall well-being.

By implementing these insights and methods, individuals can navigate the complexities of a digitally connected work environment while preserving their well-being.

Chapter 9: Raising Digital-Resilient Children

In an era where digital technology plays an integral role in children's lives from a young age, the task of raising digitally resilient children has become a paramount concern. This chapter delves into the intricate landscape of parenting in the digital age, exploring strategies to equip children with the skills, awareness, and emotional resilience needed to navigate the challenges and opportunities presented by the digital realm. From managing screen time to fostering critical thinking and online safety, the journey of raising digital-resilient children is essential to ensure that young minds engage with technology in a balanced, informed, and empowered manner.

The pervasive presence of technology in children's lives has brought about a profound impact on their cognitive, social, and emotional development. As children engage with digital devices and online platforms, it becomes imperative to understand the implications of technology on their well-being and to adopt strategies that promote a healthy and balanced relationship with technology.

The influence of technology on cognitive development is complex. On one hand, digital tools offer interactive learning opportunities that can enhance cognitive skills such as problem-solving, critical thinking, and creativity. Educational apps and digital resources can provide engaging ways for children to explore various subjects and expand their knowledge. On the other hand, excessive screen time and the passive consumption of content can impede cognitive development by limiting hands-on experiences, face-to-face interactions, and imaginative play that foster holistic learning.

The impact of technology on children's social development and mental health is also noteworthy. The digital world offers avenues for children to connect with peers, explore diverse cultures, and engage in collaborative activities. However, excessive use of social media and online interactions can lead to social isolation, comparison, and even cyberbullying. Children's self-esteem and emotional well-being can be affected by the pressures of portraying an idealized online persona or by encountering negative experiences online.

Furthermore, the potential for addictive behaviors associated with technology use warrants consideration. The dopamine-driven reward system that digital interactions can trigger in children's brains can lead to compulsive screen time and detachment from real-world experiences. This may impact their ability to regulate emotions, handle stress, and engage in activities that promote mental well-being.

By implementing strategies that promote mindful and responsible tech habits, adults can guide children in developing a balanced and empowered relationship with technology.

1. Model Healthy Tech Behavior:

Children often emulate the behaviors of adults in their lives. Model healthy tech habits by setting aside dedicated screen-free times, engaging in face-to-face interactions, and demonstrating responsible use of digital devices. Your actions send a powerful message about the importance of maintaining a balanced relationship with technology.

2. Establish Clear Screen Time Guidelines:

Set clear and age-appropriate guidelines for screen time. Discuss the purpose of screen time, such as educational content, creative expression, and entertainment, while emphasizing the importance of physical activity, social interactions, and outdoor play.

3. Prioritize Quality Content:

Encourage children to engage with high-quality, age-appropriate content that aligns with their interests and curiosity. Co-view and co-play with your children to guide their choices and foster meaningful discussions about the content they consume.

4. Create Tech-Free Zones:

Designate certain areas in your home as tech-free zones, such as the dining room or bedrooms. These spaces provide opportunities for face-to-face interactions, relaxation, and undistracted sleep.

5. Foster Open Communication:

Create an environment where children feel comfortable discussing their digital experiences, challenges, and concerns. Encourage open conversations about online safety, responsible behavior, and the potential impact of technology on their emotions and well-being.

By following these strategies, parents and caregivers can play an active role in cultivating digital resilience and well-being in the younger generation. Nurturing mindful tech habits from a young age sets the foundation for a balanced and empowered relationship with technology, equipping children to navigate the digital world with confidence, awareness, and a sense of agency.

Chapter 10: Technology-Assisted Mental Health

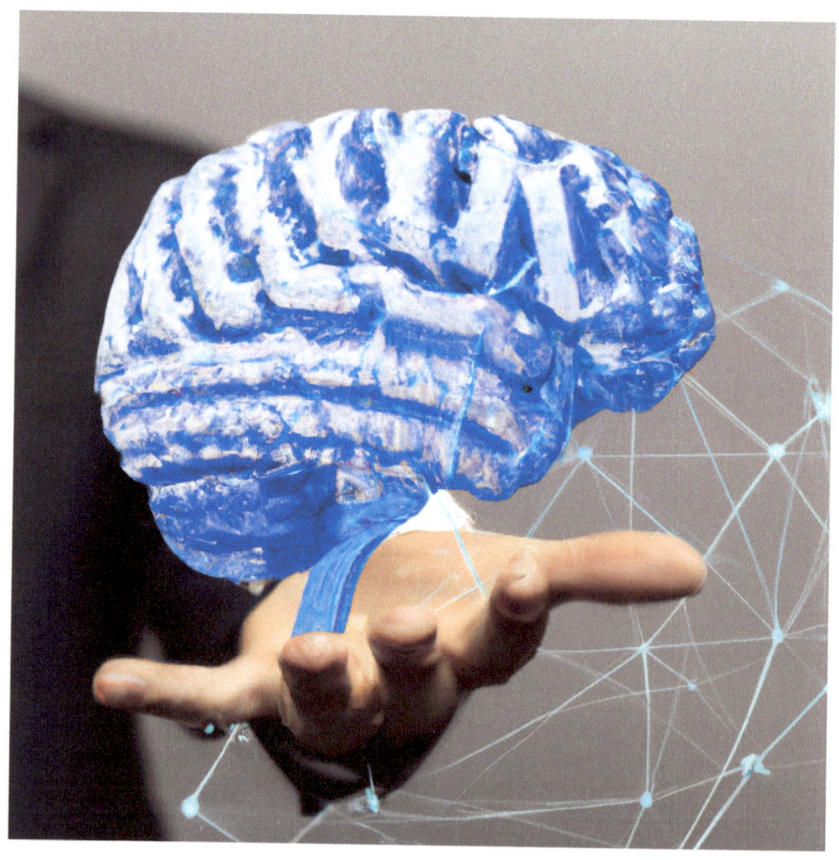

The intersection of technology and mental health has ushered in a new era of accessibility and innovation in the field of psychological well-being. This chapter delves into the transformative potential of technology-assisted mental health solutions, exploring the diverse range of tools and platforms that are shaping the way individuals access support, coping strategies, and interventions for mental health challenges. From therapy apps to virtual reality experiences, the integration of technology in mental health care offers novel opportunities to enhance access, reduce stigma, and empower individuals on their journeys toward emotional resilience and psychological well-being.

The digital landscape has given rise to a plethora of tools and platforms that are revolutionizing mental health support and intervention. These innovative solutions leverage technology to make mental health resources more accessible, personalized, and effective, catering to a wide range of needs and preferences.

From therapy apps that offer on-demand access to licensed therapists via text, audio, or video sessions, to virtual support groups that connect individuals facing similar challenges, technology has democratized access to psychological support. Notable examples include platforms like Talkspace and BetterHelp, which provide users with a convenient and confidential way to engage in therapy, particularly valuable for those with busy schedules or limited access to in-person therapy.

Virtual reality (VR) has also emerged as a promising avenue for mental health intervention. VR experiences simulate real-world scenarios that help individuals confront and manage anxiety, phobias, and stress. For instance, individuals with social anxiety can engage in VR scenarios that gradually expose them to social situations, allowing them to build confidence and practice coping strategies in a controlled environment.

Mindfulness and meditation apps offer individuals tools to manage stress, anxiety, and improve overall well-being. These apps guide users through meditation sessions, breathing exercises, and relaxation techniques, fostering self-awareness and emotional regulation. Apps like Headspace and Calm have gained popularity for their user-friendly interfaces and curated content.

Artificial intelligence (AI) and machine learning are also being harnessed to provide personalized mental health insights and interventions. AI-powered chatbots offer a nonjudgmental space for individuals to express their thoughts and feelings, offering immediate support and suggesting coping strategies. Woebot, for example, engages users in conversations, provides psychoeducation, and helps individuals track their moods over time.

Moreover, technology-assisted mental health solutions extend beyond apps and platforms. Online communities and forums provide spaces for individuals to connect, share experiences, and receive support from peers facing similar challenges. These communities can help reduce feelings of isolation and provide a sense of belonging, fostering a sense of solidarity among those navigating mental health journeys.

While technology-assisted interventions offer unprecedented accessibility and convenience, they also raise concerns about privacy, efficacy, and the preservation of the therapeutic relationship.

Benefits:

Accessibility: Technology breaks down geographical barriers, making mental health resources accessible to individuals regardless of their location. For example, individuals residing in remote areas or those with mobility challenges can access therapy and support through online platforms, widening the reach of mental health care.

Reducing Stigma: Online interventions can mitigate the stigma associated with seeking help for mental health concerns. Individuals who may be hesitant to attend in-person therapy due to perceived stigma can find solace in the anonymity and privacy afforded by digital platforms.

Personalization: Technology enables personalized interventions by analyzing user data to tailor content and strategies to individual needs. AI algorithms can adapt interventions based on user feedback, offering a tailored experience that aligns with the user's progress and preferences.

Immediate Support: Therapy apps and chatbots offer immediate support when individuals are in distress, providing coping strategies and resources outside of traditional therapy hours. This can be particularly valuable during crisis situations.

Cost-Effectiveness: Technology-assisted interventions often come at a fraction of the cost of in-person therapy, making mental health support more affordable and accessible to a broader population.

Potential Drawbacks:

Lack of Human Interaction: The absence of face-to-face interactions in digital interventions can diminish the therapeutic relationship and the nuances of nonverbal communication. This may affect the depth of connection between the user and the intervention.

Privacy and Security: Technology use raises concerns about the security and confidentiality of sensitive mental health data. Ensuring the privacy of user information is paramount to prevent data breaches and protect individuals' personal information.

Efficacy and Regulation: The efficacy of technology-assisted interventions varies widely. While some interventions have demonstrated positive outcomes, others may lack rigorous scientific validation. Regulating the quality and effectiveness of these interventions is essential to ensure users receive evidence-based support.

Dependency on Technology: Excessive reliance on technology for mental health support may hinder the development of natural coping mechanisms and interpersonal skills. Balancing technology use with face-to-face interactions remains crucial for holistic well-being.

Digital Divide: Not all individuals have equal access to technology and reliable internet connections, creating a digital divide in accessing mental health care. Socioeconomic disparities can impact the accessibility and effectiveness of technology-assisted interventions.

In conclusion, the integration of technology into mental health care presents both opportunities and challenges. As technology continues to shape the landscape of mental health support, it is essential to carefully evaluate the benefits and potential drawbacks, considering individual preferences, needs, and ethical considerations to harness the full potential of technology while safeguarding user well-being.

Chapter 11: Ethical Considerations in Digital Well-Being

In an era marked by rapid technological advancement and pervasive digital interactions, the ethical dimensions of digital well-being emerge as a critical facet of our relationship with technology. This chapter delves into the complex web of ethical considerations surrounding digital well-being, exploring the responsibilities of individuals, technology creators, policymakers, and society at large. From issues of data privacy and algorithmic bias to the ethical design of digital platforms, the exploration of ethical frameworks in the context of digital well-being is essential to ensure that technology serves as a tool for empowerment, enrichment, and human flourishing.

As technology becomes increasingly intertwined with our pursuit of well-being, it is essential to critically examine the ethical implications that underlie these interventions.

Informed Consent and Autonomy: Digital interventions often require individuals to share personal data and engage with algorithm-driven recommendations. Ensuring informed consent becomes crucial to respect individual autonomy. For instance, a mental health app that collects user data should transparently communicate how the data will be used and empower users to make informed choices about their participation.

Data Privacy and Security: The collection, storage, and sharing of user data in digital interventions raise concerns about data privacy and security. Developers must prioritize robust security measures and provide clear guidelines on how user data will be protected. For instance, a fitness app that tracks user activity should have stringent data encryption and user-controlled data sharing settings.

Algorithmic Bias and Fairness: Digital interventions often rely on algorithms to deliver personalized recommendations. Ensuring these algorithms are free from bias and promote equitable outcomes is crucial. A mindfulness app that tailors content based on user demographics should ensure that algorithmic decisions do not perpetuate stereotypes or discrimination.

User Empowerment and Agency: Digital interventions should empower users to take charge of their well-being journey. Designing interventions that prioritize user agency and choice allows individuals to customize their experiences to align with their preferences and values. For example, a nutrition app should offer diverse dietary options rather than promoting a one-size-fits-all approach.

Long-Term Impact: The long-term effects of digital interventions on well-being should be carefully considered. While short-term benefits may be evident, understanding the potential implications on mental, emotional, and social aspects is crucial. A mental health app designed to alleviate stress should also assess its impact on overall life satisfaction and relational well-being.

Transparency and Accountability: Ethical digital interventions require transparency about their intended outcomes, limitations, and potential risks. Developers should also be held accountable for the ethical implications of their interventions.

A well-being platform should clearly communicate its approach, methodology, and any potential conflicts of interest to users.

In conclusion, as digital interventions for well-being become an integral part of our lives, addressing the ethical implications becomes paramount.

Chapter 12: Sustaining Digital Well-Being in the Future

As technology continues its rapid evolution, the quest to sustain digital well-being takes center stage in our collective journey. This chapter explores the dynamic landscape of digital well-being, delving into strategies and principles that individuals, communities, and society can adopt to ensure a harmonious and enriching relationship with technology in the face of ongoing advancements. From cultivating digital mindfulness to advocating for responsible technology development, the pursuit of sustaining digital well-being is a call to align technology's trajectory with human values, ethical considerations, and the timeless imperative of holistic flourishing.

The ever-evolving landscape of technology has propelled humanity into uncharted territories, redefining the way we interact, work, and live. As we reflect on this journey, it becomes evident that technology's impact on well-being is both multifaceted and continually evolving. From the advent of the internet to the rise of artificial intelligence, each technological milestone has brought new opportunities and challenges to the forefront of our well-being considerations.

As we navigate this landscape, it's essential to acknowledge that technology is neither inherently good nor inherently harmful. Its impact on well-being is shaped by how we wield it, the intentions behind its development, and the choices we make in its use. The integration of technology has enabled unprecedented access to information, communication, and services, yet it has also introduced novel stressors and complexities. Balancing the benefits with the potential drawbacks requires vigilance, adaptability, and an ongoing commitment to informed decision-making.

Moreover, technology's ongoing impact on well-being extends beyond the individual level to encompass societal and global dimensions. The rapid dissemination of information and the interconnectivity afforded by technology have transformed how we engage with social issues, advocate for change, and respond to crises. While technology has amplified our collective voice and facilitated positive change, it has also exposed vulnerabilities in privacy, security, and the potential for manipulation. Reflecting on these dynamics prompts us to consider not only the immediate impact of technology on well-being but also the long-term consequences that ripple through our societies and shape our collective future.

In navigating the complex relationship between technology and well-being, several key takeaways emerge as guiding principles for individuals and societies alike. First, the concept of balance stands paramount. Striking a balance between digital engagement and offline experiences is vital for preserving mental clarity, meaningful connections, and overall well-being. While technology enriches our lives, it's essential to consciously allocate time for activities that foster creativity, face-to-face interactions, and introspection.

Furthermore, the pursuit of digital well-being requires a commitment to continuous learning and adaptability. The technological landscape is dynamic, with new devices, platforms, and trends emerging regularly. Staying informed and proactive allows individuals to harness technology's benefits while adapting to changes that may challenge their well-being. Additionally, nurturing digital resilience equips individuals to cope with setbacks, adapt to digital disruptions, and maintain emotional equilibrium in the face of constant change.

To sustain digital well-being, it's imperative for society to foster an environment of responsible technology development. This entails advocating for transparent data practices, equitable access to digital resources, and the incorporation of well-being considerations in the design of digital platforms. By promoting ethical and human-centered technology, we can collectively shape a digital landscape that aligns with our values and fosters well-being on a societal level.

In conclusion, the journey of digital well-being is a continuous exploration, an ongoing quest to harmonize technology's potential with the pursuit of holistic flourishing. By embracing balance, mindfulness, continuous learning, and ethical responsibility, individuals and societies can navigate the ever-changing technological landscape with resilience, purpose, and a steadfast commitment to well-being.

Conclusion: Forging a Flourishing Digital Future

As we bring this exploration of digital well-being to a close, it's evident that the path to a flourishing digital future requires deliberate choices, thoughtful approaches, and a profound understanding of the intricate interplay between technology and humanity. This journey has taken us through the evolving landscapes of digital engagement, offering insights into how technology shapes our well-being individually and collectively.

The principles of balance, mindfulness, continuous learning, and ethical responsibility that we've uncovered remain vital pillars in our pursuit of a harmonious coexistence with technology. Just as the pioneers of science, philosophy, and art stood at the forefront of human progress, we too stand at the intersection of innovation and well-being, equipped with the tools to guide technology's trajectory for the greater good.

In a world shaped by rapid technological evolution, we must remember that our values, intentions, and choices steer the course of progress. The digital landscape will continue to unfold with unprecedented opportunities and challenges, demanding that we remain vigilant in our quest for understanding, prosperity, and the reduction of unnecessary suffering.

As we embrace the future, let the wisdom of history's greatest minds and the insights of modern thinkers guide us. Just as Aristotle contemplated the essence of life and Galileo unveiled the secrets of the cosmos, we too have the capacity to shape a destiny where technology enhances our lives, expands our horizons, and uplifts our collective well-being.

Let us forge ahead with purpose and resilience, always mindful of the impact our choices have on ourselves, our communities, and the world at large. By adhering to the principles of mindful digital engagement and responsible technology development, we pave the way for a future in which humanity thrives amidst the boundless potential of the digital age.

In closing, may our relentless pursuit of understanding, prosperity, and well-being continue to be the driving force behind every technological stride we take. As we embark on this journey, let us never forget that our capacity for growth, compassion, and conscious choice remains the beating heart of the digital era.

Epilogue: Embracing the Uncharted Horizons

As we draw the final curtain on this exploration of the digital landscape and its profound impact on our well-being, we find ourselves at the threshold of endless possibilities and uncharted horizons. The journey we've undertaken has illuminated the intricate dance between technology and humanity, offering insights that will undoubtedly shape our path forward.

From the musings of philosophers and scientists to the creations of artists and innovators, our collective history has been defined by the relentless pursuit of understanding and growth. The digital age represents a new chapter in this grand narrative—one where the fusion of human ingenuity and technological prowess propels us to heights previously thought unreachable.

As we navigate the complexities of this era, let us be guided by the wisdom of those who came before us and the visionaries who walk among us. Our capacity to harness technology for the betterment of society and the elevation of well-being rests not solely on the innovations we create, but on the values and ethics that underpin their development and use.

Just as the cosmos beckoned astronomers and the canvas inspired artists, the digital realm beckons us—a new generation of explorers—to chart its unexplored territories. With every line of code, every innovation, and every choice we make, we are shaping the legacy of this era for ourselves and generations to come.

In closing, let us approach the future with a sense of responsibility and a commitment to fostering well-being in all its dimensions. By embracing the principles of understanding, prosperity, and the reduction of suffering, we can ensure that our journey through the digital landscape is one of empowerment, growth, and fulfillment.

With unwavering determination and a dedication to our core values, we embark on the next chapter of our story—one that will undoubtedly be shaped by the interplay of human creativity, technological innovation, and the pursuit of a better world for all.

Copyright:

The Digital Equilibrium :

Navigating Technological Advancement for Optimal Well-Being

Kindle Direct Publishing

First edition [2023]

www.ingramcontent.com/pod-product-compliance
Lightning Source LLC
Chambersburg PA
CBHW040757240526
45474CB00008B/91